D1307179

SEATTLE
MARINERS

by Lew Freedman

Published by ABDO Publishing Company, 8000 West 78th Street, Edina, Minnesota 55439. Copyright © 2011 by Abdo Consulting Group, Inc. International copyrights reserved in all countries. No part of this book may be reproduced in any form without written permission from the publisher. SportsZone™ is a trademark and logo of ABDO Publishing Company.

Printed in the United States of America,
North Mankato, Minnesota
112010
012011

 THIS BOOK CONTAINS AT LEAST 10% RECYCLED MATERIALS.

Editor: Chrös McDougall
Copy Editor: Nicholas Cafarelli
Interior Design and Production: Carol Castro
Cover Design: Christa Schneider

Photo Credits: Morry Gash/AP Images, cover; John Froschauer/AP Images, 1, 8, 11, 43 (middle); Tony Dejak/AP Images, 4; Elaine Thompson/AP Images, 7; AP Images, 12; Gene Smith/AP Images, 15; B Bennett/Getty Images, 17, 42 (top); John Swart/AP Images, 18; Barry Sweet/AP Images, 21, 23; Rick Stewart /Allsport, 25; FILE/AP Images, 26, 47; Bill Chan/AP Images, 29, 32, 43 (top); Nick Wass/AP Images, 31, 42 (bottom); Jeff Zevelansky /AP Images, 35; Jim Bryant /AP Images, 36, 42 (middle); Jeff Chiu /AP Images, 39; Gail Burton/AP Images, 41, 43 (bottom); Bill Kostroun/AP Images, 44

Library of Congress Cataloging-in-Publication Data
Freedman, Lew.
  Seattle Mariners / by Lew Freedman.
     p. cm. — (Inside MLB)
  Includes index.
  ISBN 978-1-61714-059-4
  1. Seattle Mariners (Baseball team)—History—Juvenile literature. I. Title.
  GV875.S42F74 2011
  796.357'6409797772—dc22
                              2010038742

TABLE OF CONTENTS

CHAPTER 1

THE GREATEST SEASON

Baseball players often say that the best feeling in the world is coming out to the ballpark knowing you have a good chance of winning that day. In 2001, just about every day felt like that for the Seattle Mariners and their fans.

The magic of the 2001 season was put in motion in 1999, when the team opened Safeco Field. It was immediately considered one of the best ballparks in all of baseball. Safeco Field routinely sold out in 2001. Approximately 3.5 million fans came out to watch the Mariners play that year. And they had a lot to cheer about.

One of the highlights was Ichiro Suzuki, a 27-year-old rookie from Japan. He had been a star player in Japan before coming to Seattle and the American League (AL).

The player who became known simply as Ichiro was a fan favorite right away with his dazzling catches in right field. But it was his batting and base

Right fielder Ichiro Suzuki helped turn the 2001 Seattle Mariners into baseball's top team during the regular season.

running that really set him apart. He stunned the baseball world by batting an AL-best .350 and collecting 242 hits during his first season. With incredible speed on the base paths, Ichiro was routinely able to bunt for hits and steal bases. In fact, he stole 56 bases in his first year—another AL best.

Ichiro combined with a veteran lineup to make the Mariners one of Major League Baseball's (MLB) best hitting teams that season. They led the AL in several batting categories, including team batting average and runs batted in (RBIs).

Second baseman Bret Boone was a breakout star in 2001. He hit .331 with an AL-best 141 RBIs. First baseman John Olerud, designated hitter Edgar Martinez, and center fielder Mike Cameron were also key middle-of-the-order batters.

The Mariners' pitching staff was among the best in baseball. As a team, they had the lowest earned run average (ERA) and gave up the fewest hits in the AL. Starting pitchers Freddy Garcia and Jamie Moyer anchored the veteran pitching staff. Jeff Nelson was one of the most reliable relief pitchers in baseball. They all threw to Dan Wilson, a strong defensive catcher.

Mariners' second baseman Bret Boone enjoyed a career year in 2001, hitting 37 home runs and driving in 141 runs.

The team also had an experienced leader. Manager Lou Piniella had already led the Cincinnati Reds to a World Series title. He was one of the most respected managers in baseball.

With all those pieces in place, the Mariners had one of the best regular seasons in MLB history. In fact, their 116 wins tied an MLB record that was nearly 100 years old. The only other team to win that

8 SEATTLE MARINERS

many games in one season was the 1906 Chicago Cubs.

The Mariners easily won the AL West Division and qualified for the playoffs. Expectations were high for Seattle's first World Series title.

The Mariners opened the Division Series of the playoffs against the Cleveland Indians. The series turned into a major battle. The favored Mariners lost the first game, 5–0. Then they came back to win the second game. But Seattle lost the third game by a shocking score of 17–2.

Only then did the Mariners straighten things out. They won the next two games to advance to the second round of the playoffs. The fans were relieved, but the playoffs were not about to get any easier in the AL

Championship Series (ALCS). To advance to the World Series, the Mariners would have to beat the New York Yankees in a seven-game series.

The Yankees were always a very strong team. But the Mariners felt they had the weapons to beat the Yankees and win the AL pennant. However, the Mariners' dream season soon came

Jamie Moyer

The Mariners' best pitcher during the 2001 season might have been a veteran left-hander named Jamie Moyer. The 38-year-old tied for second in the AL with a 20–6 record. His 3.43 ERA was the sixth best in the league. Unlike many of the best starting pitchers, Moyer did not throw very hard. He specialized in throwing a mix of slower tosses, such as change-ups, curveballs, and other pitches. Moyer pitched for more than 10 years in Seattle. In 2010, at age 47, he was still a starting pitcher for the Philadelphia Phillies.

Mariners' pitcher Jamie Moyer won 20 games in 2001.

THE MAN FROM JAPAN

At home in Japan, Ichiro Suzuki could not walk down the street without being surrounded by adoring fans asking for his autograph. However, upon his arrival in the United States, Ichiro was largely unknown. As accomplished as he was, he was nervous making the change to a different culture to play in the majors.

"It was a decision that put my baseball career on the line, that's for sure," he said.

Ichiro had won batting titles in Japan, but he knew the best baseball in the world was played in the United States. He wanted to see if he could measure up. That question was answered right away. Ichiro was an instant star. Not only did he win the AL batting title as a first-year player, he was voted AL Rookie of the Year and Most Valuable Player (MVP) that season, a very rare combination.

to a disappointing finish. The Yankees beat the Mariners in five games to advance to the World Series. The one highlight for Mariners fans was a 14–3 win in Game 3 at Yankee Stadium. Boone, Jay Buhner, and Olerud all hit home runs in the win.

The third season at Safeco Field ended in disappointment. After 25 seasons, the Mariners still had not experienced a World Series. But for those who lived through it, the glow of the Mariners' 2001 season will never wear off.

Ichiro congratulates Mike Cameron after Cameron's two-run homer against the Cleveland Indians in Game 2 of the AL Division Series.

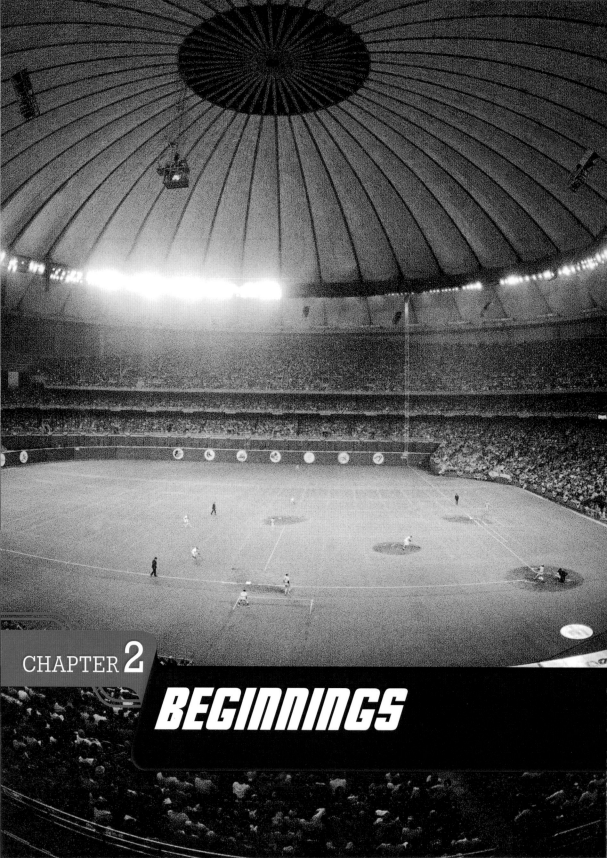

CHAPTER 2

BEGINNINGS

The Mariners were not the first MLB team to play in Seattle. The Seattle Pilots actually began playing in the AL in 1969. They played in a renovated minor league ballpark called Sick's Stadium. But the Pilots only attracted 677,944 fans that season. With such low attendance, the Pilots left Seattle after one season and became the Milwaukee Brewers.

Local baseball fans and government officials were mad when the Pilots abandoned Seattle so quickly. In 1970, they sued MLB. Several major league teams talked about moving to Seattle, but no team made the switch. The case finally went to court in 1976. At the end of a 20-day trial, the AL agreed to give Seattle a new team.

Before the team took the field, the owners had fans turn in suggestions for the team's nickname. Around 15,000 fans submitted approximately 600

More than 57,000 fans showed up for the Mariners' first game at the Kingdome in 1977.

different possibilities. The owners selected the Mariners.

The Mariners also got a new stadium. The King County Multipurpose Domed Stadium, which fans called the Kingdome, opened in 1976. It would also serve as the home for the National Football League's Seattle Seahawks.

The Kingdome was part of a new generation of stadiums that had domed roofs. This ensured that no games would be rained out—something especially important in rainy Seattle. The Kingdome could hold nearly 60,000 fans for a baseball game.

The Mariners were an expansion team that season. That meant the team was starting from scratch. For the most part, expansion teams are made up of players that other teams feel they no longer need. The new teams select many of these players in an expansion draft. Since the existing teams protected their best players and did not allow them to be drafted, the Mariners had to choose from a list of unprotected players. The team was not expected to have a winning first season.

The Mariners took the field for their first game on April 6, 1977. They lost to the California Angels 7–0 in front of 57,762 fans. It was not until the

The First Best Player

He had an average-length career—playing parts of nine seasons in the majors—and he was never a superstar. But Lee Stanton was the best player the Mariners had day in and day out during the team's first season. Stanton, a 6-foot-1, 195-pound outfielder from South Carolina, had previously played for the California Angels and New York Mets. He played in 133 games for the Mariners that first season and led the team with 27 home runs and tied for the team lead with 90 RBIs while batting .275.

Mariners first baseman Juan Bernhardt takes a pickoff throw during a 1978 game against the Baltimore Orioles.

third game of the season that the Mariners got their first win. In front of only 11,845 fans in the Kingdome, second baseman Larry Milbourne doubled home the winning run in the bottom of the ninth as the Mariners beat the Angels 7–6.

For Seattle baseball fans, the 1977 season was not solely judged by the team's wins and losses—after all, they were an expansion team. Many people in Seattle were just excited to have a major league team back in their city.

But the Mariners did do their share of losing during their first season. They finished 8–16 in April, their first

THE VOICE OF THE TEAM

Actor Danny Kaye, one of the Seattle Mariners' original owners, wooed Dave Niehaus to be the team's play-by-play radio broadcaster for its first season in 1977. He was still behind the microphone more than 30 years later in 2010.

The man who brings the action into living rooms around the region is considered the best known and most popular figure connected to the team. Niehaus has outlasted everyone else in Seattle, from owners to players to coaches to managers. With a professional style that has earned him the Ford C. Frick Award and a place in the National Baseball Hall of Fame, Niehaus tells it like the fans want to hear it. He employs a mixture of enthusiasm and truth. When Niehaus sees something remarkable unfold on the field, the signal to his audience is the phrase, "My, oh my." He called his 5,000th Mariners game during the 2009 season.

month in existence. Their worst month, however, was August. The Mariners went a lowly 6–22. The Mariners ended their first season with a record of 64–98. They finished sixth out of seven teams in the AL West Division.

Lee Stanton was the best hitter on the team that year with a .275 average. He also tied first baseman Dan Meyer for the club lead in RBIs with 90. In the record books, it was largely a forgettable baseball season in Seattle. But unlike the one-year wonder Seattle Pilots, the Seattle Mariners were here to stay.

Outfielder Ruppert Jones awaits a pitch at the Kingdome during the 1977 season. He was the team's first All-Star.

CHAPTER 3

THE BAD OLD DAYS

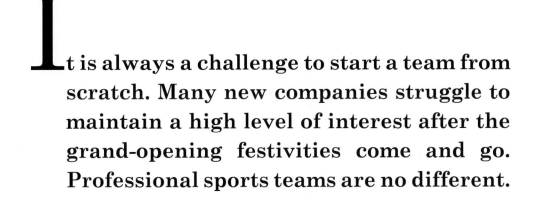

I
t is always a challenge to start a team from scratch. Many new companies struggle to maintain a high level of interest after the grand-opening festivities come and go. Professional sports teams are no different.

Expansion teams do not start from a position of strength. The process of building a title contender takes years. That means the fans must wait patiently. That was the case for the Seattle Mariners.

The Mariners attracted 1,338,511 fans to the Kingdome during the 1977 season. However, as the team continued to struggle on the field, attendance quickly dropped. The Mariners had a losing record in every season from 1977 through 1990.

The worst record during that stretch was the 56–104 finish during the 1978 season.

Pitcher Gaylord Perry had won two Cy Young Awards before joining the Mariners in 1982. He won his 300th game as a Mariner.

Gaylord Perry

Right-handed pitcher Gaylord Perry was selected to the National Baseball Hall of Fame. But he was near the end of his career when he threw for the Mariners in 1982 and 1983. Because he was 43 when he arrived, Perry earned the nickname "The Ancient Mariner," referring to the name of a famous poem.

Perry was a five-time All-Star who also won the Cy Young Award twice. Although his best years were with the San Francisco Giants and the Cleveland Indians, Mariners fans did get to witness a special occasion. On May 6, 1982, Perry won his 300th game in front of 27,000-plus fans in the Kingdome.

The Mariners did not do much better when they lost 103 games in 1980 and 102 games in 1983. Their best record during those first 14 seasons was in 1987, when they finished 78–84.

At a time when the Mariners struggled to win games, first baseman Alvin Davis's presence on the field gave the team some credibility. He was a respected player who was both a solid fielder and hitter.

Davis won the AL Rookie of the Year award in 1984. He was the first Mariners player to win that award. That year he slugged 27 home runs and drove in 116 runs. Davis was the most dependable player during those early years, earning the nickname "Mr. Mariner." He spent eight of his nine major league seasons with Seattle, retiring after one additional season with the California Angels.

During those losing years, Seattle baseball fans cheered for little things. They had to take pride in outstanding one-game showings or season-long individual performances.

Alvin Davis waves to the Kingdome crowd after hitting a home run against the Detroit Tigers in 1984.

In 1977, outfielder Ruppert Jones was Seattle's first All-Star. In September 1985, Davis was manning first base in an extra-inning game against the Cleveland Indians. There were a lot of ground balls that day, and Davis recorded 22 putouts in the game. He did it again against the New York Yankees in May 1988, tying the MLB record for a nine-inning game.

Another memorable day was May 9, 1986. Davis went 3-for-4 and drove in eight runs against the Toronto Blue Jays. That set a team record for RBIs in a game. Two of those hits were home runs as the Mariners cruised to a 13–3 win.

Although the Mariners struggled on the field during many of those early years, they did have some success in the annual draft. Since new teams often lack star players, they look to the draft to build a strong future. So the Mariners set out to draft the most talented high school and college players and then develop them in their farm system. The odds are high against drafting a player who will make it all the way to the major leagues. But the Mariners did a good job identifying prospects.

The first player Seattle took in the 1977 amateur draft was Dave Henderson. Nicknamed "Hendu," the outfielder joined the Mariners in 1981.

Mariners first baseman Alvin Davis holds New York Yankees base runner Rickey Henderson on first during a 1985 game.

He played parts of six seasons with the team and had a productive 14-year career.

The Mariners selected Jim Presley in 1979. He was a future All-Star. In 1981, the Mariners selected pitcher

Alvin Davis

For his career, Alvin Davis had a .280 batting average, hit 160 home runs, and had 683 RBIs in 1,206 games. Years later, when the Mariners created a team hall of fame, Davis was the first player inducted.

MARINER MOOSE

In 1990, as the worst days of losing on the field seemed to be past, Mariners management tried to think of ways to become more fan friendly. One idea was to add a mascot. The Mariners held a contest that encouraged children 14 and under in the Pacific Northwest to suggest what kind of mascot they should adopt. After 2,500 entries were received, the winner was chosen. The new symbol was a moose. A fifth grade student from Ferndale, Washington, was credited with selecting it. The Mariner Moose made its debut on Opening Day 1990.

The big-eared creature appears at home games and other events in the Seattle region. The Mariner Moose can often be seen trotting around the field carrying a Mariners flag. The Moose is always upbeat, but he had one particularly bad day in 1995 when he crashed into an outfield wall and broke an ankle during a game against the New York Yankees.

Mark Langston. As a rookie in 1984, he went 17–10 for the Mariners. Langston had a 16-year career in the majors after playing his first five-plus seasons for the Mariners.

In the 1980s, the Mariners added infielder Spike Owen and pitcher Bill Swift. Then, they had a major breakthrough in the 1987 draft. With their top pick that year, the Mariners selected Ken Griffey Jr. He was fresh out of high school and not quite ready for major league play. But in the years to come, he would become the Mariners' first superstar. More than 20 years later, he retired as one of the most beloved players in team history.

Pitcher Mark Langston won 74 games and had a 4.01 ERA during six seasons in Seattle.

CHAPTER 4

WINNERS AT LAST

After many disappointing seasons, the 1991 Seattle Mariners at last put together a winning record. The team finished the season 83–79. Fans were so happy to see a winner that more than 2 million went to games at the Kingdome that season.

Through shrewd drafting and smart trades, the Mariners had built a lineup that scared opposing pitchers. They already had second baseman Harold Reynolds, designated hitter/third baseman Edgar Martinez, right fielder Jay Buhner, and first baseman Alvin Davis. In 1989 they had added shortstop Omar Vizquel, too. That gave the Mariners budding stars all over the field. But the anchor of the offense was young outfielder Ken Griffey Jr.

Griffey was a speedy outfielder. But he was more feared at the plate. He threatened to get on base every time he came up to bat. Whether it was

Ken Griffey Jr. follows through on his swing at the 1990 All-Star Game at Wrigley Field in Chicago. The young player was known as "The Kid."

stroking a single or bashing a deep home run, Griffey could do it all.

Griffey was only 19 years old when he played his first major league game in 1989. He quickly rose to become one of the best—and most popular—players in baseball. During the 1990s, he led the AL in home runs four times. Fans loved that he always seemed to play with a smile on his face. Many people believed that Griffey would become one of the greatest players of all time, and he proved them right.

Griffey had an advantage over most while growing up in Cincinnati, Ohio. He had a major league player as his own tutor—his father, Ken Griffey Sr. The older Griffey was an excellent player. He played mostly with the Cincinnati Reds and the New York Yankees. Griffey Sr.'s advice helped the player called "Junior" make it to the big leagues at a younger age than most players.

Griffey Sr. joined the Mariners for the final season and a half of his career. During the 1990 and 1991 seasons, Griffey Jr. and Griffey Sr. became the first father and son to play on the same MLB team together. They also once hit back-to-back home runs in a game.

"My dad taught me that there's three parts [to playing baseball]," Griffey Jr. said. "There's hitting, there's defense, and there's base running. And

Ken Griffey Jr., *left,* and Ken Griffey Sr. kid around on the bench during a 1990 game. The father and son played together in 1990 and 1991.

as long as you keep those three separated you're going to be a good player. . . . You can't take your hitting to the field, and you can't take your base running to the plate."

During his long career, Griffey Jr. hit more than 600 home runs and was considered a lock for the Hall of Fame from an early age. But during his career, Griffey tried to stay humble.

"If I'm compared to Babe Ruth or Willie Mays, that's great," he said. "But I'm just going out there to be myself. My name is not 'The Best Player in Baseball.' My name is George Kenneth Griffey Jr."

Along with one of the best batters in baseball, the Mariners also had one of the best pitchers. Standing 6-foot-10, Randy Johnson was one of the tallest baseball players in history. With a 100 miles-per-hour fastball and a devastating slider, the man nicknamed "The Big Unit" could strike out just about anybody.

The Mariners traded for Johnson in 1989. Through 1994, he had already been to three All-Star Games and had twice finished among the top three in AL Cy Young voting. Behind Griffey, Martinez, and Johnson, Seattle had a season to remember in 1995.

The Mariners had largely been a losing team with poor attendance for most of their history. There had been rumors

The Big Unit

During his 10 years in Seattle, Randy Johnson was one of the best pitchers in the AL. He won the 1995 Cy Young Award and was in the top five in strikeouts seven times. Johnson retired after 22 seasons in 2009. He retired as a five-time Cy Young winner, a co-MVP of the 2001 World Series, and a 10-time All-Star. He pitched a perfect game in 2004. In all, he finished with a 303–166 record and 4,875 strikeouts—the second most of all time.

during the 1995 season that the team might be moved to another city. When the Mariners fell 13 games behind the California Angels at one point, it looked like another doomed season. In early September, the Mariners still looked headed for second place in the AL West. They were six games behind the Angels and running out of time. Then they got hot.

Pitcher Randy Johnson was an intimidating presence on the mound for nearly 10 seasons in Seattle. He struck out 2,162 batters from 1989 to 1998.

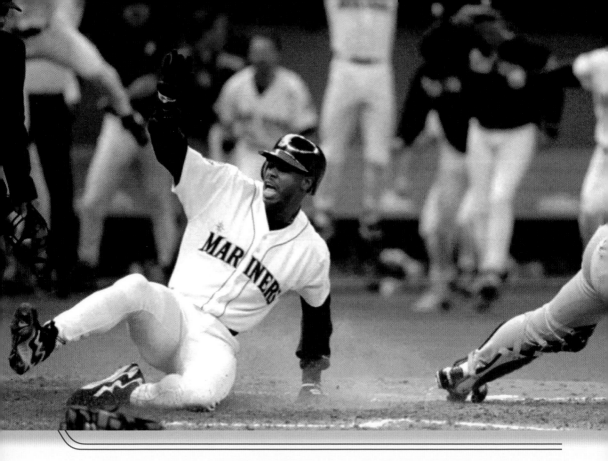

Ken Griffey Jr. crosses home plate in the bottom of the 11th inning of the 1995 AL Division Series. The run sent the Mariners on to the ALCS.

Griffey, Johnson, and their teammates put together one of the most thrilling three-week stretches in Seattle baseball history. They won 15 of their last 20 games to tie the Angels for first place. The only way to decide which team could go on to the AL playoffs was to play an extra game.

Johnson pitched for the Mariners. He struck out 12 batters in the 9–1 victory that gave Seattle its first division title. The Mariners were headed to the playoffs for the first time.

Some people wondered if the Mariners would have enough energy left to beat the Yankees in the AL Division

Series (ALDS). After losing the first two games in New York, the Mariners won the next two at home. It all came down to a decisive Game 5.

Tied 4–4 in the ninth inning, Seattle turned to Johnson. Although he had started Game 3, Johnson came out of the bullpen on this night. He held the Yankees scoreless in the ninth, and then again in the 10th. But in the 11th, the Yankees took a 5–4 lead.

Seattle had one more chance in the bottom of the inning. Leadoff hitter Joey Cora reached first on a bunt single. Then Griffey hit a single up the middle, advancing Cora to third. Martinez stepped to the plate with a chance to drive in the tying run. Instead, he did more than that. Martinez blasted a double down the left-field line, scoring Cora and Griffey.

A-ROD

Alex Rodriguez could go down as one of the greatest players to ever play the game. His historic career began in Seattle. The Mariners selected the high school player from Miami, Florida, with the first pick in the 1993 draft. He had planned to attend the University of Miami, but instead signed with the Mariners. He spent one year in the minor leagues and then moved right in as a starting shortstop in Seattle.

Rodriguez became an instant star. He quickly became one of the game's top hitters and was a serious MVP contender. When his contract expired after the 2000 season, Rodriguez was one of the game's top all-around players. Although he said he would like to stay in Seattle, the Texas Rangers made him such a big offer that he felt he had to take it. When Rodriguez agreed to a 10-year, $252 million contract with Texas, it was the richest for any player in any sport.

Griffey flashed his trademark smile as he slid into home plate for the winning run. In Seattle, the play became known simply as "The Double."

The underdog Mariners then moved on to play the Cleveland Indians in the ALCS. But the happy season ended there. The powerful Indians won in six games and advanced to the World Series.

Any worries about relocation were put to rest after that 1995 season. The Mariners' playoff run had given Seattle baseball fever. When the Mariners made their charge, attendance grew to more than 50,000 per game. Soon the local government agreed to help pay for a new stadium that would open in 1999.

On the field, the Mariners missed out on the 1996 playoffs. But 1997 turned into another strong season. Griffey

Safeco Field

When Safeco Field opened during the summer of 1999, the Mariners finally had a shiny new ballpark to call their own. At the Kingdome, some fans were unhappy because the Mariners played indoors and on artificial turf, not in the sun on green grass. With a retractable roof, Safeco Field offered the chance to play under cover when it rained and under blue sky when it was nice out. The field cost $517.6 million to build and seated 47,116 people when it opened.

was again among the AL leaders in most batting statistics. Shortstop Alex Rodriguez was emerging as one of the league's best players, too. Meanwhile, Johnson was putting together a dominant season. He even had two games in which he struck out 19 batters. The MLB record is 20.

Despite their strong season, the Mariners lost to the Baltimore Orioles in four games in the ALDS.

Alex Rodriguez watches as the ball sails over the outfield wall for a solo home run during the 2000 playoffs.

Mariners fans would have little to cheer about in the upcoming seasons, however. Over the years, Griffey, Johnson, and Rodriguez all left Seattle. Johnson was traded to the Houston Astros during the 1998 season. Griffey left for his hometown Cincinnati Reds after the 1999 season. After finishing third in the AL MVP voting and leading the Mariners to another ALCS, Rodriguez left for the Texas Rangers following the 2000 season.

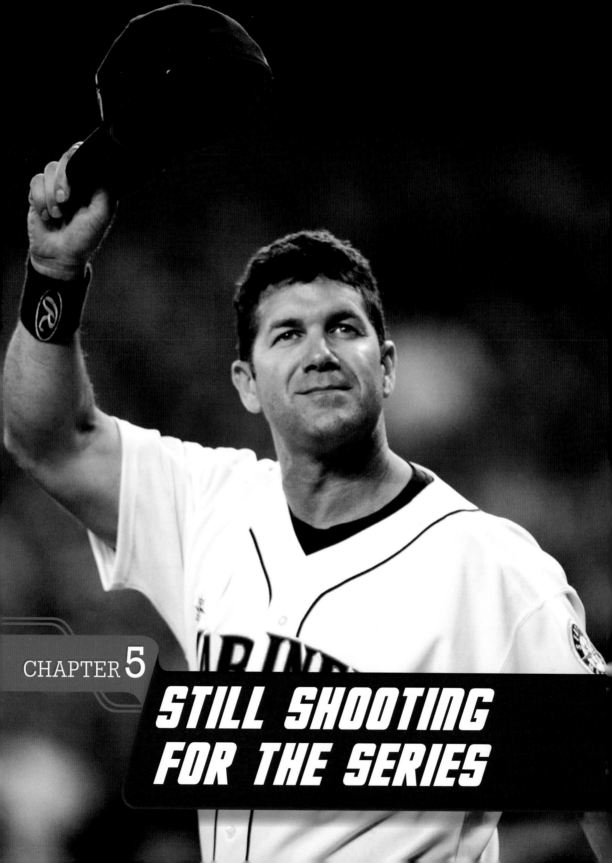

CHAPTER 5

STILL SHOOTING FOR THE SERIES

The Mariners were able to maintain some success after their dream 116-win season in 2001. The team won 93 games in each of the next two seasons. But after that, the team went into another slump.

Manager Lou Piniella had joined the Mariners in 1993. The fiery manager stayed in Seattle after his three biggest stars left. But after the 2002 season, he too left the Pacific Northwest. Piniella joined the Tampa Bay Devil Rays for the 2003 season.

The one star who remained in Seattle for his whole career was Edgar Martinez. The 41-year-old wanted to continue his career in 2005. But he felt he was slowing down and could no longer help the team the way he had over the years. He retired after the 2004 season.

"It is hard, very hard," he said of retiring. "I feel in my mind and my heart I want to keep playing. But my body is

Mariners designated hitter Edgar Martinez tips his hat to the crowd during "Edgar Martinez Day" in 2004.

Immortalized

When popular designated hitter Edgar Martinez retired after the 2004 season, his 18 years of service with the Seattle Mariners was honored in an unusual way. The city of Seattle named a street after him. South Atlantic Street was renamed Edgar Martinez Drive. The 6-foot, 175-pound Martinez finished his career with 309 home runs, 1,261 RBIs, and a batting average of .312. A seven-time All-Star, Martinez was presented with the Roberto Clemente Award for his humanitarian service to the community. Following his retirement, MLB also named its annual best designated-hitter award after him.

saying something differently, so I feel this is a good decision."

Since Martinez retired, Ichiro Suzuki has emerged as Seattle's new superstar and fan favorite. When he arrived from Japan in 2001, nobody knew if his talents would translate to MLB. But the fleet-footed outfielder became a routine All-Star.

In 2004, Ichiro became the single-season hit king. He tied George Sisler's single-season record of 257 hits during the first inning of a game against the Texas Rangers on October 1. He then broke Sisler's 84-year-old record with a line drive up the middle in the third inning. Ichiro ended with 262 hits that season. Through 2010, he has won two batting championships.

Before the 2010 season, Ichiro had recorded more than 3,000 hits, counting his time in both Japan and the United States. That is a milestone that only the best and most consistent players reach.

"There are two important elements in batting," Ichiro said. "There's a part of you that needs to be aggressive and a part that needs to be patient. These are contradictory elements, but unless you can be

Ichiro records his 258th hit of the 2004 season in a game against the Texas Rangers, breaking George Sisler's 84-year-old record.

both, there'll be an imbalance in your batting."

Although the Mariners were struggling to win games, the team debuted another star in 2005. A 19-year-old pitcher named Felix Hernandez pitched 84.1 innings with a 2.67 ERA. He established himself as a top pitcher in the next

seasons, even earning the nickname "King Felix." By 2009, he was an All-Star and finished second in the AL Cy Young vote.

Behind the strong play of Ichiro and Hernandez, the Mariners had a good season in 2009. Hernandez was 19–5 with a 2.49 ERA. Ichiro batted .352 and led the league in

THE KID

Some people credit Ken Griffey Jr. with saving baseball in the Pacific Northwest. When he arrived in Seattle as a teenager in 1989, the Mariners were a losing team. After hitting a home run in his first at-bat in the Kingdome, Griffey quickly began to change that atmosphere. The player nicknamed "The Kid" played 1,535 games in Seattle and hit 398 home runs before leaving after the 1999 season. He was also the AL MVP in 1997.

While Mariners fans loved his production at the plate, they also loved his personality. Griffey was often seen wearing a backward hat and a big smile. He genuinely seemed to enjoy playing the game. Injuries late in his career slowed down his production, but Griffey still finished with 630 home runs—fifth all time. The Kid returned to Seattle in 2009 to much fanfare. He retired in June 2010 after 22 seasons.

hits. The 2009 season also saw the return of Ken Griffey Jr. After nine years in Cincinnati and part of one season with the Chicago White Sox, he returned to the Mariners to much fanfare. He even blasted 19 home runs. Although the Mariners finished 85–77, they still finished third in the AL West and missed the playoffs.

By 2010, they were back to their struggling ways. Early in the season, Griffey announced that he was retiring after 22 seasons. The Mariners were rebuilding once again. However, after Hernandez won the 2010 AL Cy Young Award, fans hoped the team would soon reach its first World Series.

Ken Griffey Jr. watches his hit during a 2010 game against the Baltimore Orioles. Griffey came back in 2009 to end his career as a Mariner.

TIMELINE

1976	On November 5, the expansion Seattle Mariners choose their new team through an expansion draft.
1977	The Mariners play their first regular-season game on April 6, losing 7–0 to the California Angels before 57,762 fans at the Kingdome.
1977	On April 8, the Mariners win the first game in team history, 7–6, over the Angels.
1982	While pitching for the Mariners, right-handed pitcher Gaylord Perry wins his 300th game on May 6, 1982, 7–3 over the New York Yankees.
1987	Eventually considered by many to be the best designated hitter of all-time, Edgar Martinez begins his 18-year major league career as a third baseman.
1989	Outfielder Ken Griffey Jr., not yet 20 years old, makes the Mariners' roster out of spring training and makes his major league debut on April 3. Randy Johnson is acquired from the Montreal Expos and makes his Mariner debut.
1991	After 14 straight losing seasons, the Mariners record their first winning season, finishing 83–79.
1994	Alex Rodriguez makes his first appearance in the majors, playing in 17 games at shortstop as a late-season call-up.

1995	Coming from behind to catch the Angels in the standings in late September, the Mariners win their first division title to qualify for the playoffs for the first time. The Mariners defeat the Yankees in a five-game series before losing to the Cleveland Indians.
1997	The Mariners win the West Division for a second time after completing the regular season with 90 victories. Griffey leads the AL with 56 home runs. Johnson finishes the year 20–4, his first 20-win season.
1998	For the second year in a row, Griffey hits 56 homers and leads the AL.
1999	The Mariners start the season playing in the Kingdome, but play their final game there on June 27 before moving into their new ballpark. The $517.6 million Safeco Field hosts its first Mariners game on July 15.
2001	The Mariners put together one of the greatest regular-season performances of all-time, tying the major league record of 116 wins set by the Chicago Cubs in 1906. Japanese newcomer Ichiro Suzuki, who wins the Rookie of the Year and MVP awards, sparks the Mariners. The Mariners best the Cleveland Indians in the ALDS, but lose to the Yankees in the ALCS.
2009	After an absence of nine years, Griffey returns to the Mariners to complete his major league career in the place he started. He retires midway through the 2010 season.

QUICK STATS

FRANCHISE HISTORY

Seattle Mariners (1977–)

WORLD SERIES

None

AL CHAMPIONSHIP SERIES
(1977–)

1995, 2000, 2001

DIVISION CHAMPIONSHIPS
(1977–)

1995, 1997, 2001

WILD-CARD BERTHS

2000

KEY PLAYERS
(position[s]; seasons with team)

Bret Boone (2B; 1992–93, 2001–05)
Jay Buhner (OF; 1988–2001)
Alvin Davis (1B; 1984–91)
Freddy Garcia (SP; 1999–2004)
Ken Griffey Jr. (OF; 1989–99,
    2009–10)
Felix Hernandez (SP; 2005–)
Randy Johnson (SP; 1989–98)
Mark Langston (SP; 1984–89)
Edgar Martinez (3B/DH; 1987–2004)
Jamie Moyer (SP; 1996–2006)
Harold Reynolds (2B; 1983–92)
Alex Rodriguez (SS; 1994–2000)
Ichiro Suzuki (OF; 2001–)
Dan Wilson (C; 1994–2005)

KEY MANAGERS

Darrell Johnson (1977–80):
    226–362
Lou Piniella (1993–2002):
    840–711, 15–19 (postseason)

HOME FIELDS

Kingdome (1977–99)
Safeco Field (1999–)

* Statistics through the 2010 season

"The other guys, all they have to do is use their big butts and big python arms to hit homers. Me, I'm the little guy in the group. People always root for the little guy."—Ken Griffey Jr., who had 630 home runs during his career.

On May 2, 2002, Mariners outfielder Mike Cameron tied a major league record by hitting four home runs in one game against the Chicago White Sox.

"I just don't have that first-step explosion anymore."—Mariners manager Lou Piniella joked after he tripped and fell charging up the dugout steps to protest an umpire's call.

"The funniest part is that the carpet is smoldering, the smoke is rising, we're laughing and Lou glances back like 'Oh,' tells us to 'shut up,' and keeps right on talking. It smelled like dead cats in there after that."—Pitcher Chris Bosio, after manager Lou Piniella went into a post-game rage and kicked over the food table, starting a fire with the overturned Sterno cans while players tried to put it out by pouring milk over the flames.

"I wouldn't be surprised if it was Leon Roberts."—Mariners manager Maury Wills, when asked who his starting left fielder would be. Trouble was, Roberts had been traded away five weeks earlier.

"He was just a fan, one who didn't know the game."—Mariners manager Rene Lachemann on owner George Argyros. Lachemann ripped the dugout phone out of the wall when Argyros called him during a game.

GLOSSARY

amateur draft

Once a year, major league teams take turns choosing players coming out of high school or college to sign as professionals. They draft players in the opposite order of how they finished with won-lost records to give weaker teams a chance to stock up on the best new players.

attendance

The number of fans at a particular game or who come to watch a team play during a particular season.

contender

A team that is in the race for a championship or playoff berth.

designated hitter

A position used only in the American League. Managers can employ a hitter in the batting order who comes to the plate to hit instead of the pitcher.

expansion

In sports, the addition of a franchise or franchises to a league.

farm system

A big-league club's affiliate teams in the minor leagues, where players are developed for the majors.

pennant

A flag. In baseball, it symbolizes that a team has won its league championship.

prospects

Young players, usually ones who have little major league experience.

putout

When a batter hits the ball in play, but the ball is caught in the air or the batter is thrown out while trying to run to a base.

retire

To officially end one's career.

retractable

Can be opened or closed mechanically depending on the weather.

FOR MORE INFORMATION

Further Reading

Arnold, Kirby. *Tales From The Mariners' Dugout*. Champaign, IL: Sports Publishing LLC, 2007.

Isaacson, Melissa. *Sweet Lou—Lou Piniella: A Life in Baseball*. Chicago: Triumph Books, 2009.

Komatsu, Narumi, and Ichiro Suzuki. *Ichiro on Ichiro*. Seattle: Sasquatch Books, 2004.

Web Links

To learn more about the Seattle Mariners, visit ABDO Publishing Company online at **www.abdopublishing.com**. Web sites about the Mariners are featured on our Book Links page. These links are routinely monitored and updated to provide the most current information available.

Places to Visit

National Baseball Hall of Fame and Museum
25 Main Street
Cooperstown, NY 13326
1-888-HALL-OF-FAME
www.baseballhall.org
This hall of fame and museum highlights the greatest players and moments in the history of baseball. Former Mariners Rich "Goose" Gossage, Rickey Henderson, Gaylord Perry, and Dick Williams are enshrined here.

Peoria Sports Complex
15707 North 83rd Avenue
Peoria, AZ 85382-3827
623-773-8720
http://www.peoriaaz.com/sportscomplex/sportscomplex_main.asp
Peoria Stadium has been the Mariners' spring-training ballpark since 1994. The San Diego Padres also train here.

Safeco Field
1250 1st Avenue South
Seattle, WA 98134-1216
206-346-4000
http://mlb.mlb.com/sea/ballpark/index.jsp
This has been the Mariners' home field since 1999. Tours are available when the Mariners are not playing.

INDEX

About the Author

Author Lew Freedman is a longtime newspaper sportswriter who has worked for the *Philadelphia Inquirer*, the *Anchorage Daily News*, the *Chicago Tribune*, and is currently sports editor of *The Republic* in Columbus, Indiana. He has also written many books about baseball. A baseball fan his entire life, Freedman attended many Seattle Mariners games at the old Kingdome and Safeco Field.